Foods of Korea

Barbara Sheen

KIDHAVEN PRESS
A part of Gale, Cengage Learning

Detroit • New York • San Francisco • New Haven, Conn • Waterville, Maine • London

© 2011 Gale, Cengage Learning

LIBRARY OF CONGRESS CATALOGING-IN-PUBLICATION DATA

Sheen, Barbara.
  Foods of Korea / by Barbara Sheen.
    p. cm. -- (A taste of culture)
  Includes bibliographical references and index.
  ISBN 978-0-7377-5115-4 (hardcover)
  1. Cookery, Korean--Juvenile literature. 2. Korea--Social life and customs--Juvenile literature. I. Title.
  TX724.5.K65S53 2010
  641.59519--dc22

                                                      2010018789

Kidhaven Press
27500 Drake Rd.
Farmington Hills MI 48331

ISBN-13: 978-0-7377-5115-4
ISBN-10: 0-7377-5115-0

Printed in the United States of America
1 2 3 4 5 6 7 14 13 12 11 10

Printed by Bang Printing, Brainerd, MN, 1 Ptg., 11/2010

Contents

The Heart of Korean Cooking

Korea is an ancient country located on a **peninsula** south of China. It was occupied by Japan during World War II. After the war, the **Allies** divided Korea into two occupied zones—one in the North and one in the South. The division was supposed to be temporary, but in 1948 two separate nations were established, the Democratic People's Republic of Korea, or North Korea, and the Republic of Korea, or South Korea. Today, South Korea is a modern, prosperous country. North Korea is a closed society to which foreign visitors are not welcome.

Despite this division, the Korean people share the same history, culture, and taste in food. No matter

RUSSIA

CHINA

NORTH
KOREA

SEA
OF
JAPAN

★
Pyongyang

Incheon ● ★
Seoul

**SOUTH
KOREA**

*YELLOW
SEA*

● Pusan

Hiroshima ●

JAPAN

Cattle
Grains
Fish
Fruit
Legumes
Pork
Potatoes
Rice
Vegetables

FOOD REGIONS OF KOREA

An Interesting History

Korean civilization dates back to around 3000 B.C. Ancient Koreans developed a complex society, which was divided into three kingdoms. Each kingdom had close ties to China, which influenced Korean culture.

The three kingdoms united in A.D. 668, but split up again in the ninth century. In 1392 one king took control. This was known as the Choson dynasty. The Choson dynasty ruled until 1910, when Japan took over Korea.

When Japan was defeated in World War II, Korea was divided into a northern and southern state. North Korea was supervised by the former Soviet Union. The United States supervised South Korea. In 1948 each state became a separate nation.

In 1950 North Korea invaded South Korea, starting the Korean War. The war involved twenty countries. Fighting continued until 1953 when a truce was declared.

what other food is served, rice, vegetables, and soybeans find their way onto Korean tables. These staples are the heart of Korean cooking.

An Essential Part of Life

Rice is essential to life in Korea. Bap (bahp), the Korean word for rice, is synonymous with food. Koreans greet each other by asking, "Have you had bap today?" This greeting probably developed during times when food was scarce. An answer of "yes" meant that the person had food, so things were good.

Bap, or rice, is an important part of Korean food. It was once even used to determine a person's wealth.

Indeed, in the past Koreans measured their wealth by how much rice they had. Chef Cecilia Hae-Jin Lee re-

Steamed Rice

Koreans are very fussy about how they make their rice. If you prefer not to soak the rice first, cook it in 3 cups of water.

Ingredients
1 cup short grain white rice
1 ½ cups of water

Directions
1. Soak the rice in warm water for 15 to 30 minutes.
2. Drain the rice. Put the rice in a large saucepan with the water.
3. Cook on high heat, uncovered, until the water boils. Stir the rice.
4. Reduce the heat to low. Cover the pot. Cook the rice until all the liquid has been absorbed, about 20 minutes.
5. Remove the pot from the stove. Keep it covered for 10 minutes.
6. Uncover the pot. Use a spoon to fluff the rice before serving.

Serves 4.

members an event from her childhood that illustrates this: "Like all Korean families, rice was as important to us as money. So, the year our apartment flooded . . . none of us questioned our mom when she began yelling at us to grab the sacks of rice and hurry upstairs."[1]

Rice is still important to Koreans. South Korean farmers grow 6.3 million tons of rice each year. Most of it is not exported, but consumed by Koreans. Every Korean eats about 198 pounds (90kg) of the grain annually. In comparison, Americans eat about 22 pounds

(10kg) of rice a year.

Not just any rice will do. Koreans prefer short-grain rice, which has a moist, sticky texture, a snow-white color, and a nutty aroma.

The Main Dish

Rice is the main dish at every meal. Meat, fish, and vegetables are eaten as side dishes that complement the rice. According to author Chang Sun-Young, "We have quite a different concept of main dishes from Westerners—the real main dishes being always rice. . . . Everything else is a side dish to help diners consume . . . [the rice] with relish [delight]."[2]

Rice is also the key ingredient in many Korean foods. It is used to make rice flour and rice vinegar. It is turned into sweet and savory rice cakes. It is rolled in seaweed for lunches and snacks. It is fried and tossed with vegetables, and it is made into juk (chook), a porridge that Koreans eat for breakfast and as a late-night snack.

Spicy Pickled Vegetables

Juk is often served with vegetables, and vegetables almost always accompany rice. Green onions, cabbage, and red chili peppers are among the most popular. Red chili, in particular, plays a key role in adding fiery flavor to Korean cooking that Koreans adore. Spicy food, they say, warms them during their cold winters and, because it makes them perspire, cools them during the summers.

Portuguese traders brought the hot peppers, which

Red chile is used to make Korean food spicy. They are used fresh, dried, as flakes, or in a paste.

originated in South America, to Korea in the seventeenth century. Koreans eat them fresh. They turn them into chili flakes, powder, and paste by drying them in the sun. According to author Hi Soo Shin Hepinstall, "In autumn the whole Korean landscape is ablaze with a blanket of red [peppers]—on thatched roofs, in front yards, on side road pavements, almost anywhere one can find an open sunny space."[3]

Korean cooks season almost every dish with chili products. Gochujang (KOH-chu-ching), chili paste, is served as a condiment with every meal. The dark-red paste is made from red chili flakes, **fermented** soybean paste, and sweet rice flour. It tastes salty, sweet, and spicy all at the same time. Gochujang, explains food writer Jane Daniels Lear, "is one of Korea's most extraordinary gifts to the . . . world. . . . We . . . stir it into everything from pot roast to soups."[4]

Kimchi

One of the most important ways Korean cooks use chili paste, powder, and flakes is in **kimchi** (KIM-chee). It is a spicy pickled vegetable dish that can feature almost any vegetable. Koreans make about 200 varieties of kimchi. But the most popular recipes feature cabbage.

Koreans have been making kimchi for 3,000 years. Originally, making kimchi was a way for Koreans to

Similarities and Differences

Korean food is similar to other Asian foods. For instance, rice is important in all Asian cooking, and soy sauce is a staple in Korean, Chinese, and Japanese cooking.

Korean cooking also has its differences. It is more dependent on fermented foods than any other country in Asia. In fact, kimchi is uniquely Korean. Moreover, Korean food is often spicier, heartier, and stronger smelling than Japanese or Chinese food.

In addition, Korean meals are served with three to twelve little side dishes known as banchan. Other Asian cuisines do not typically serve side dishes.

Kimchi

Kimchi is not difficult to make but it takes time and patience.

Ingredients
1 head Napa cabbage, cleaned and chopped
¼ cup sea salt or kosher salt
4 cups water
2 tablespoons water
1 tablespoon flour
1 tablespoon minced garlic
1 tablespoon minced ginger
1 tablespoon crushed red chili
2 green onions, chopped
2 teaspoons sugar

Directions
1. Mix the salt and water in a large nonmetal bowl. Add the cabbage. Cover the bowl with plastic wrap. Let it stand overnight.
2. Drain the cabbage, but keep the salty water.
3. Rinse the cabbage.
4. Combine the flour and 2 tablespoons water to make a paste. Add the other ingredients. Add this mixture to the cabbage. Mix well.
5. Pack the cabbage in a jar. Pour about 1/4 cup of the saltwater into the jar, leaving about 2 inches (5cm) of space on the top of the jar. Close the jar tightly. Store at room temperature for three days. Refrigerate after opening.

Depending on the size of the cabbage, makes 1 to 2 quarts.

preserve vegetables so that they would have a supply during their long winters.

November is kimjang (KIM-ching), or kimchi-making season, in Korea. During this month, Korean stores and roadside stands overflow with vegetables. Making kimchi takes time and energy. Koreans usually make dozens of jars of kimchi at a time. In fact, most Korean homes are equipped with a second refrigerator designed to store kimchi.

Often friends, neighbors, and relatives help each other make kimchi. To make cabbage kimchi, the cook salts cabbage leaves, and places them in **brine,** or salty water, for about three hours. The salt removes moisture from the cabbage without affecting its texture. Then, chili paste and spices such as chili flakes, garlic, and

Almost any vegetable can be used to make kimchi, a spicy pickled vegetable dish. It includes red chile.

green onions are rubbed on each leaf. The kimchi is then left to ferment for about three days. During this time, harmless bacteria known as **probiotics** form and kill off any dangerous bacteria that form when food spoils. When consumed, probiotics take up space in the digestive tract where harmful bacteria might otherwise settle, which helps keep people healthy.

Kimchi tastes sour and zesty, and is crisp. It has a strong aroma. Three or four different types are usually served as side dishes with every meal. It is also a key ingredient in recipes like kimchi soup, kimchi stew, and kimchi pancakes. The average Korean eats 5 to 7 ounces (0.14 to 0.20 kg) of kimchi each day. "We Koreans love it so much," says Hepinstall, "that . . . a meal without kimchi is unthinkable."[5]

Essential Seasonings

Kimchi is not the only fermented food Koreans enjoy. Koreans ferment soybeans to make kanjang (KAN-ching), or soy sauce, and toenjang (DWEN-ching), soybean paste. Koreans use both foods as condiments, in dipping sauces, and as ingredients in soups and stews. To make kanjang and toenjang, Korean cooks boil and then grind dried soybeans into a paste. They form the paste into large blocks called meju (MAY-jew), which are left outside to ferment for at least one month.

Next, they put the meju in brine. How long it is left in the brine depends on the cook. The longer it ferments, the stronger the flavor. When the meju is ready, the liquid and the solid are separated. The solid is the soy-

Sauces are an essential part of Korean cooking. Many are made of soy and used for dipping or in soups.

bean paste, which tastes sweet, nutty, tart, and salty. The liquid is the soy sauce. It is darker and sweeter than what Americans are used to.

Long ago most Koreans made their own kanjang and toenjang. In fact, it was a major yearly event. Today busy Koreans buy these products ready-made in supermarkets.

Whether homemade or store-bought, Koreans cannot do without kanjang and toenjang. Both add an earthy flavor and fragrance to Korean foods and they are rich in protein and healthy bacteria. "They," according to Hepinstall, "are primarily responsible for the character and unique flavor of Korean food."[6]

Korean food is, indeed, delicious. Soybeans, rice, pickled vegetables, and chili peppers help give it a bold and distinctive flavor. These ingredients are at the heart of Korean cooking.

A Delicious Balance

Korean cooks try to balance five elements or flavors—sweet, sour, bitter, salty, and spicy—in all their meals. They believe doing so promotes good health. "Food and medicine are from the same root. Each influences well-being,"[7] explains Sung, a Korean man.

Balancing flavors also prevents any one flavor from dominating, which enhances the taste of food. Korea's most popular dishes reflect this delicious balance. Among them are soup, little side dishes known as **banchan** (BAHN-chin), a rice dish called **bibimbap** (BEE-bim-bap), and barbecued meats.

"All Koreans Need"

Koreans love soup. No meal is considered complete without it. Unlike in the West, where soup is served before the main course, in Korea soup is eaten as part of the main course. "Soup and a bowl of rice is often all Koreans need," says Sun-Young. "A delicious soup and some well seasoned kimchi . . . can make a meal quite sumptuous. . . . Many Koreans think they have not had a proper meal if it lacks a bowl of soup."[8]

Korean soups usually start with the water rice is rinsed in. Beef, chicken, or seafood is added to the water to make a rich **broth**. Then, any number of different ingredients are added. Local favorites include meatball

Soup makes up the central piece of many Korean meals. Ginseng soup is among the most popular.

Eating Korean Style

Traditionally, Koreans eat sitting on the floor with their legs crossed at a low table, although some Koreans now use Western-style tables and chairs. Either way, the oldest person is always seated first and everyone waits until the oldest person starts eating before they, too, begin to eat. No one leaves the table until after the oldest person has left.

Korean food is not served in courses. People eat in any order they like. Each person is given a bowl of soup and a bowl of rice. All the other foods are put in the center of the table. These bowls are not passed around the table. Instead, diners take bite-size servings out of these centrally located bowls.

Koreans do not use knives or forks. They use chopsticks and spoons. Since the left hand is used for sanitary functions, even left-handed people use only the right hand for holding spoons and chopsticks.

Four women enjoy a meal together. Korean-style meals are taken seated on the floor before a low table.

soup, radish and chive soup, kimchi soup, and oxtail soup. But no matter the type of soup, Korean cooks make sure that the flavor of each ingredient balances out that of the others. And, by adding tidbits from the banchan side dishes to their soup, diners can customize the flavor to their liking.

Ginseng soup is among everyone's favorites. It features ginseng root, the root of an herb with a sweet, bitter, and spicy flavor that Koreans love. Besides its distinctive flavor, ginseng has an interesting shape. It is very similar to that of a human body. In addition, ginseng is believed to have medicinal properties that **herbalists** say strengthen the body and fight fatigue. This is why Koreans eat ginseng soup if they feel like they are catching a cold.

But that is not the only time they eat this favorite soup. In fact, ginseng soup is so well liked that there are specialty restaurants in Korea where ginseng soup is the only item on the menu.

Koreans have been eating ginseng soup since about the seventh century. Ginseng is native to Korea and grows wild in the mountains of North Korea. It is also cultivated on farms throughout Korea. Farmers plant ginseng seeds in the fall in long straight rows, which they cover with straw to protect the fragile seeds from the cold. After the ginseng is harvested, the roots are washed and peeled. Next they are steamed, then dried in the sun. This process is believed to release the herb's medicinal properties.

To make ginseng soup, Korean cooks stuff a chicken with cooked rice, dates, chestnuts, and salt. The bird is placed in rice water to which ginseng root, garlic, white pepper, and green onions are added. The chicken is cooked until the meat is fall-off-the-bone tender.

Before the soup is served, the chicken is cut into pieces. Little bowls of salt, pepper, and red chili powder accompany the soup to the table. The end result is a perfect harmony of flavors and textures that Koreans typically eat with loud smacking sounds and slurps, which in Korea is considered a way to show food is appreciated.

Little Side Dishes

As with soup, banchan—three to twelve little side dishes that are served with almost every meal—provides Korean diners with a collection of flavors. Banchan can include different types of kimchi, savory fish cakes or pancakes, dried anchovies cooked with chili paste, boiled potatoes seasoned with soy sauce, spinach or mushrooms topped with sesame oil and garlic, sliced radishes, bean sprouts salad, or pickled garlic, to name just a few.

Banchan is typically served in little bowls placed in the center of the table, which everyone shares. Diners pick out bits with long thin metal chopsticks and add the tasty

A number of banchan dishes make up a traditional Korean meal.

Spicy Spinach

This vegetable dish is a popular banchan side dish. It is not difficult to make. Whole leaf, chopped, or baby spinach can be used

Ingredients
6 ounces spinach
1 tablespoon soy sauce
½ teaspoon sugar
1 teaspoon minced garlic
1 teaspoon sesame seeds
1 ½ teaspoons sesame oil
½ teaspoon crushed red pepper

Directions
1. Cook the spinach in boiling water for 1 minute.
2. Remove the spinach. Put in a colander and rinse the spinach with cold water.
3. Squeeze the water out of the spinach. Put the spinach in a bowl.
4. Combine the other ingredients. Mix well. Pour over the spinach and mix.
Serves 2.

morsels to their soup or rice. Koreans say that sharing food in this manner brings them closer together. "It's really neat," says John Bagdonas, an American who spent four years in Korea "There's an intimate, communal feel."[9]

Banchan is always mixed with the main dish. "A single banchan isn't meant to be eaten alone; it's a way of balancing the many tastes and textures in a Korean meal. It's a part of a whole,"[10] explains Jonathan Frye, whose mother is Korean. This ensures a balance of flavors.

A Classic Rice Bowl

Bibimbap also provides Korean diners with a collection of flavors. This bowl of rice topped with a large variety of ingredients is probably the most popular lunch dish in Korea. And, it is a common way for Koreans to use leftovers.

Bibimbap starts with a bowl of sweet white rice. Beef, mushrooms, and a wide range of cooked vegetables such as spinach, bean sprouts, **kelp**, squash, and carrots are arranged in a flowery pattern on top of the rice and topped with a cracked raw or fried egg. But there is no exact recipe. Pork or seafood may be used in place of beef, and almost any vegetable may be added. The ingredients are seasoned with soy sauce, sugar, garlic, green onions, pepper, and sesame seeds. Kanjang along with other banchan is served on the side. Before eating, Koreans vigorously mix the ingredients.

This bowl of bibimbap is topped with a fried egg. This dish is a popular way to use leftovers.

In fact, the name bibmbap comes from the stirring sound. Writer Kristin Johannsen describes her experience eating bibambap in Korea: "The bibambap was spectacular. Even after we stirred and mashed the ingredients together in approved fashion, the delicate flavors of the individual vegetables and the sweetly spicy accent of pepper came through clearly. It was truly a lunch to remember."[11]

Grilled at the Table

Other favorite dishes like **bulgogi** (BOOL-gah-jee), thin strips of beef, and **kalbi** (GAWL-bee), beef ribs, are cooked right at the table. But first they are marinated for hours in a sauce made from sesame oil, garlic, soy sauce, black pepper, green onions, sugar, chili powder, and ginger. The marinade makes the already-tender meat buttery soft. The meat is cooked on a metal platter atop a small gas grill that in restaurants is usually built right into the table, and in homes is set on the table. The cook snips the kalbi off the bone with scissors before placing it on the grill.

When the meat is done, diners pick it off the grill with their chopsticks and wrap it in a lettuce leaf. They add banchan tidbits, a bit of rice, toenjang or gochujang, and a sliver of green onion. Then, they pop the whole thing into their mouth and eat it in one bite.

In the royal court of the Choson dynasty, which ruled Korea from 1392 until 1919, the meat was presented with tiny bamboo skewers secured on each end to enhance its appearance. But even without the skewers, Koreans consider kalbi and bulgogi to be their finest dishes. Inviting guests to a kalbi or bulgogi dinner in one's home or taking guests out to a barbecue restaurant is considered a special treat. Koreans adore the

Bulgogi

Bulgogi is easy to make. You can broil the meat or cook it on an outdoor or indoor grill.

Ingredients

1 ½ pounds beef sirloin cut into thin slices, ⅛– to 1–inch thick
½ cup soy sauce
1 tablespoon sesame oil
1 tablespoon minced garlic
2 tablespoons sugar or honey
1 tablespoon sesame seeds
1 teaspoon ground ginger
1 teaspoon crushed red pepper
2 green onions, minced
1 head leaf lettuce, leafs washed and separated (optional)
3 cups cooked rice (optional)

Directions

1. Combine all the ingredients (except the beef, lettuce, and rice) in a large bowl. Mix well.
2. Add the beef to the bowl. Refrigerate for at least one hour.
3. Put the meat on a hot grill or in a broiler pan sprayed with nonstick cooking spray. Cook until the meat is browned.
4. Bulgogi can be served with lettuce leaves and rice on the side, so that diners can wrap the meat in the leaves with a bit of rice.

Serves 4.

Bulgogi is cooked in the middle of the table at this Korean restaurant.

Hotpots

Hotpot cookery is quite popular in Korea. Hotpots are stews that are cooked at the table. Traditionally, they are made in stone pots that are placed on a ring heated with charcoal.

Koreans make many different varieties of hotpots. Most contain a large number of ingredients. There are hotpots that feature vegetables, pork, beef, and seafood.

To make a hotpot, the cook cuts up all the ingredients in advance. Then, broth combined with garlic, red pepper flakes, soy sauce, and sesame oil is heated in the hotpot. Next, the other ingredients are added. When the food is piping hot, each diner is served an individual bowl of the cooking liquid. Using chopsticks, diners pick out whatever tasty tidbits they prefer from the hotpot, which they dip into the bowls of hot liquid.

combination of flavors in these dishes, which, according to chef and author Jamie Purviance, taste "warm and cold, mild and pungent, raw and cooked—all at once. . . . Cold and sweet ingredients temper those that are warm and spicy. Subtle and briny flavors elevate what's sour and intense."[12]

Clearly, when flavors complement and enhance each other, food tastes delicious. Korean cooks have mastered the art of balancing different flavors, ensuring the good taste of Korea's favorite dishes.

Chapter

3

A Snacker's Paradise

Korea is a snacker's paradise. Food stalls and carts, known as **pojangmachas** (PAH-ching-may-chas), line city streets. Mouthwatering aromas fill the air, luring everyone from businessmen to children to stop for a fast, tasty, and inexpensive snack. According to reporter Cathy Rose A. Garcia, "Seoul [South Korea's capital] is a city that never stops eating. Walk around the streets of Seoul, and you'll find street food stands always surrounded by people eating different kinds of snacks all day long. . . . Pojangmachas start setting up business around early afternoon and stay open until 11 P.M. Every night, office workers, students, and tourists walk down the busy street. More often than not, they'll

This food stall in Seoul sells sausage to a passerby. Pojangmachas offer a variety of inexpensive foods.

end up seduced by the appetizing sight and smell of Korean snacks being cooked at the pojangmachas."[13]

Every pojangmacha has its own specialty. Some offerings are sweet and some are savory. Everything is delicious.

Carp Bread

Bungeoppang (PUNG-yah-bang), or carp bread, is a popular sweet treat. It is a fish-shaped pastry made with red bean paste. Fish-shaped pastries do not have a long history in Korea. The Japanese introduced the pastries during the time they occupied Korea. Red beans, on the other hand, have been grown in Korea since 1000 B.C. Koreans boil the beans with sugar then mash them into a thick sweet paste that they use to fill all sorts of pastries in much the same manner that chocolate is used in the United States. However, the beans, which are loaded with vitamins, minerals, protein, and fiber, have more nutritional value than chocolate.

To make bungeoppang, cooks pour batter made from sweet rice flour into a fish-shaped mold similar to a waffle iron. Next they add a layer of red bean paste. They seal the bean paste inside the pastry with another layer of batter. Finally, they close the mold, and the pastry, which is about as large as a slice of bread, is cooked until it is crisp on the outside and chewy on the inside. "They're quite tasty, hot and filling,"[14] says public radio reporter Matthew Bell.

There is also a version made in the shape of a flower, which is popular in the springtime, and an ice cream

Other Popular Snacks

Sundae (SOON-day) is a popular Korean snack. It is a dark-colored sausage made by stuffing pigs' intestines with a mixture of vegetables, noodles, spices, and pigs' blood. It is steamed and cut into small pieces. Sundae is accompanied by salt mixed with chili flakes.

Twigim (TEE-ghim) is another common snack. It is flour-battered and deep-fried vegetables and seafood. Mandu (MAN-doo) is also fried. Mandu is a dumpling filled with ground beef or pork, bean sprouts, green onions, garlic, and ginger.

Kimbap (KIM-bahp), too, is very popular. It is Korean-style sushi in which anything and everything is wrapped in little seaweed rolls. Rice, spicy vegetables, ham, beef, and cheese are just a few of the many fillings.

Kimbap, Korean-style sushi, is wrapped in seaweed.

version, in which ice cream replaces the bean paste. In this version, the ice cream is added after the pastry is cooked.

A Sweet Treat

Hotteok (HAH-tee-ah-kuh) is another sweet favorite. It is a pancake stuffed with brown sugar, cinnamon,

Korean Dipping Sauce

Most any food can be dipped in this sauce. It can also be used to marinate beef, chicken, or tuna steak. You can decrease or increase the amount of chili flakes and garlic, depending on your taste.

Ingredients
5 tablespoons soy sauce
2 tablespoons sesame oil
1 teaspoon sugar
1 teaspoon crushed red pepper
1 teaspoon crushed garlic
1 teaspoon sesame seeds
1 green onion minced

Directions
Combine all the ingredients. Mix well.
Makes ¼ cup of sauce.

black sesame seeds, and nuts. Hotteok can have other fillings, too. Some versions are quite colorful. In one type the dough is flavored with green tea, which gives the pancake a greenish color. In another, the pancake is filled with juicy raspberries, which turns the treat pink.

Hotteok originated in China. Nineteenth-century Chinese **merchants** brought it to Korea. Koreans liked the sweet treat. It soon became a local favorite.

To make hotteok, Korean cooks make dough from

a mixture of wheat, rice, and corn flours, yeast, sweet peas, sugar, and water. After the dough rises, it is filled with sugar and nuts. Then it is pressed into a large, flat circle with a special tool, and is either deep fried, or baked on a griddle, which makes for a healthier snack. Either way, the pancake is cooked until it is crisp and golden brown on the outside and hot and gooey inside. It is eaten right out of the pan when it is still steaming hot.

In fact, it takes some skill to keep the hot filling from squirting out. Food blogger Robyn Lee describes her experience: "The filling will just come out when you least suspect it. . . . After taking a mostly goo-less bite, about 99 percent of the filling squirted out onto my shirt. Not only is this stuff burning hot, but if you are not careful it will shoot out at you. . . . Of course . . . fried hotteok is worth the trouble. . . . Sweet, spicy, nutty, and crunchy; this is good stuff." [15]

Savory Pancakes

Other pancakes are savory rather than sweet. These pancakes not only are favorite snacks, they are also served as a side dish at meals. **Pajeon** (PAY-chen), or green onion pancakes, are among the most popular. To make pajeon, cooks create a thin batter made of wheat and rice flour, water, eggs, and chopped green onions. The batter is cooked in a skillet, much like American pancakes. Pajeon, however, is quite a bit larger. In fact, pajeon is often called Korean pizza, because it is about as large and thick as a small pizza, and because it can

A woman fries savory pancakes. These are often served as side dishes at meals or as snacks.

be topped with many different foods. Seafood pajeon, for instance, is a popular choice. To make it, the cook sprinkles clams, shrimp, chopped squid, or other sea-food on top of the batter in the pan. The cook flips the pajeon as it cooks, so that both sides brown. When it is ready, the pajeon is cut into slices. It is served with a multi-flavored dipping sauce that combines chili flakes, soy sauce, rice vinegar, garlic, and sugar.

Pajeon is so tasty that when South Korea's First Lady, Kim-Yoon-ok, visited New York City in 2009, she cooked and served the green onion pancakes to a group of Korean War veterans. "I wanted to give them a new taste of Korea as something positive and delicious," she explains. "From the war they do not have many pleas-ant food memories."[16]

Snacks on a Stick

Other savory snacks are wrapped around a stick. Odeng (OH-deng), a Korean-style fish cake, is one of the most popular of these snacks. Cooks make odeng by mix-ing ground white fish and flour, wrapping the mixture around a wood skewer, and boiling it in a spicy broth.

Odeng is served with a cup of the broth. Koreans dip the odeng into the broth, which moistens the fish cake and adds a zesty flavor. If any broth remains when they finish the odeng, they drink the broth up. Condiments like soybean and chili paste are also provided, as are little brushes to "paint" the fermented pastes onto the fish cake.

Odeng vendors do not charge patrons for the snack

Food from the Sea

Seafood is readily available and popular in Korea. The Noryangjin Fish Market in Seoul is a popular place to buy seafood. At 216,535 square feet (66,000 sq. m.) it is almost as large as four football fields laid end to end. It houses 700 vendors selling fresh seafood from 15 different Korean ports.

Here there are hundreds of fish tanks filled with live edible sea creatures such as oysters, abalone (an oyster-like shellfish), clams, squid, eels, lobsters, shrimp, scallop, jellyfish, octopus, which vary from thumb size to gigantic, and fish like red snapper, tuna, sea bream, carp, cod, and flounder, to name just a few. Shoppers can buy seafood whole or have the vendors cut and clean their purchase.

Koreans grill fish and seafood. They add them to porridge, soups, and stews. They also eat them raw.

This Korean food store in Seoul sells dried seafood, like the octopus being held aloft.

Snacks on a stick, such as fish, are popular in Korea. They are often sold at ponjangmachas.

until after they have finished eating. Koreans take as many sticks of odeng as they want without paying. When they finish eating, the vendor counts the sticks and charges diners accordingly. Although snackers could walk away without paying, most Koreans would not think of doing such a dishonorable thing. So, this system works well. According to the writing team at

Pajeon

These pancakes are not difficult to make. In fact, you can get a ready-made mix much like American pancake mixes in Asian grocery stores. This recipe makes the batter from scratch. Serve the pancakes with the dipping sauce recipe given in this chapter.

Ingredients
1 cup flour
1 cup water
1 beaten egg
4 green onions, cut into small pieces
oil for cooking

Directions
1. Combine all the ingredients except the oil. Mix well. It should be the consistency of a thin pancake batter. If it is too thick, add a little more water. Let it stand for about 10 minutes.
2. Heat enough oil in a frying pan to thinly cover the bottom of the pan over medium heat. Pour in half the batter. Tilt the pan, so the batter spreads to form a thin sphere.
3. Cook until the bottom is golden brown, about 3 to 4 minutes. With a wide spatula, flip the pancake over and cook the other side.
4. Put the pancake on a plate. Add more oil, if needed. Repeat the process with the rest of the batter.

Serves 2.

ZenKimchi, an online Korean food journal, "Odeng is pretty good unless you don't like sea food. It tastes similar to sweet imitation crab meat. . . . It's a great street snack on a chilly winter day. . . . The method for eating odeng on the street is something I'm still trying to get used to. In other countries . . . you go up to the vendor, pay the money, the vendor gives you your order. At odeng stands, a patron walks up to the vendor, grabs a stick of odeng and starts eating without even talking to the vendor. . . . Basically, you tell the vendor how many you ate, or the vendor looks at the number of sticks next to you."[17]

Odeng, pajeon, bungeoppang, and hotteok are just a few of the many snacks that ponjangmachas have to offer. There are also skewered grilled chicken, spicy rice cakes, ramen noodles, crispy deep-fried vegetables, tasty dumplings, and hot dogs wrapped in pastry, to name just a few. With so many yummy snacks to choose from, busy Koreans cannot resist stopping for a quick bite to eat.

Meaningful Foods

Koreans love to celebrate. Holidays and special events are a time for families to get together and enjoy special foods with symbolic meaning.

Becoming a Year Older

Koreans celebrate New Year's Day twice. Once on January 1, and then again when the New Year begins on the traditional lunar calendar, which has been used in Asia for centuries. **Sol-nal** (SOL-nay), or Lunar New Year's Day, is Korea's biggest holiday. It is the start of a new year, the first day of spring, and the day on which every Korean's age is calculated. Everyone in Korea is considered one year older on Sol-nal.

The date of Sol-nal changes annually based on the

A Korean family shares a ceremonial meal together on Sol-nal. Food plays an important role in celebrating the Lunar New Year.

cycles of the moon, but the way it is celebrated does not. Sol-nal festivities begin first thing in the morning when Koreans put out food on a special table to honor their dead ancestors. The exact foods differ, but they are usually grouped by color. Once the food is out, each family member bows to their ancestors. Then the children bow to older living family members.

Now it is time for the traditional breakfast feast. It features ttokguk (TEH-teh-gook), a thick beef broth topped with steamed rice cakes and bits of green onions. According to Korean tradition, a person cannot become a year older without eating the soup. In fact, when Koreans ask each other's age they often ask how many bowls of ttokguk the other has eaten? Chef Cecilia Hae-Jin Lee recalls: "The best part of Soll [Sol-nal] for me was sneaking into the kitchen . . . and peering into a huge pot of rice cake soup boiling over the fire. I would . . . inhale the aroma of the steaming soup while salivating with anticipation until one of the women discovered me and chased me out of the kitchen. . . . Each year, when the women would serve up the hot bowls . . . Uncle Number 5 would inevitably say that we were 'eating another year.'"[18]

Symbolic Cakes

The rice cakes in the soup are not like the packaged rice cakes sold in the United States. Koreans have been making rice cakes for thousands of years. Archeologists have found Korean grinding stones, used to make rice flour, and steamer baskets, used to steam rice cakes, dating back more than 2,000 years.

Koreans make many different types of rice cakes. Those used in ttokguk are thin snow-white ovals made of rice flour and water. They are steamed until they are pillowy soft. Bland and

Songpyeon are half moon-shaped rice cakes used to celebrate the autumn harvest festival. Pine needles are used in the cakes.

sticky, they pick up the beefy flavor of the broth they swim in. Many cooks add dumplings and slivers of beef and egg to the soup

According to chef Lee, Sol-nal "is a time to sweep away the misfortunes of the previous year and look forward to new endeavors."[19] Koreans say that eating ttokguk helps this to happen. Good luck, they believe, sticks to the sticky cakes. Their round shape stands for the sun, which symbolizes strength in the new year, while the clear soup represents a clear, untroubled mind in the year to come.

Korean Thanksgiving

Rice cakes are also an important part of the **Chuseok** (CHU-see-uk), a three-day harvest moon festival that is often called Korean Thanksgiving. It occurs in August around harvest time when the full moon is at its brightest and highest point. During Chuseok, Koreans give thanks for the season's harvest. And, they always eat **songpyeon,** (SONG-pie-ee-en), half-moon-shaped rice cakes that have special meaning and a very interesting aroma.

To make the cakes, cooks combine rice flour and hot water to make smooth dough, which they roll into little balls. They use their thumbs to make an indentation in the balls, which they fill with a sweet paste made of red beans, crushed sesame seeds, or chestnuts. They then form the cake into a half-moon shape while sealing in the filling. The little half moons are placed in an earthenware steamer sandwiched between layers of

Spiced Potatoes

This potato dish is a popular side dish for any occasion. It is simple to make. It can be served hot or chilled like potato salad.

Ingredients
2 medium potatoes, washed, cut into small pieces
2 tablespoons soy sauce
1 teaspoon minced garlic
1 tablespoon sesame seeds
1 tablespoon sesame oil
2 green onions, chopped

Directions
1. Put the potatoes in a saucepan with water to cover. Bring the water to a boil, cook until the potatoes are tender.
2. Combine all the other ingredients, mix well.
3. Drain the potatoes.
4. Put the potatoes in a bowl. Pour the sauce over the potatoes. Mix well.

Serves 4.

freshly picked pine needles. The pine needles form a feathery pattern on the rice cakes, which are cooked until they are hot and chewy. They also give the cakes a lovely woodsy scent, and a delicate flavor. "Whenever I think of this rice cake," Hepinstall says, "the fragrance of pine needles always floats past my nose."[20]

Koreans have been using pine needles in this way for centuries. They say that steaming the rice cakes on a layer of pine needles purifies the body and imparts good luck. Pine needles do contain chemicals that are believed to fight disease and can induce a feeling of calm.

Korean cooks take great pride in their songpyeon. In fact, in the past, Koreans said that if a woman made beautiful songpyeon, she would have beautiful children. If she did not, her children would be ugly.

Birthday Celebrations

Although Koreans add another year to their age on New Year's Day, they still celebrate their birthdays. No Korean birthday celebration is complete without muyokguk (MY-yah- kuh-guk), or seaweed soup.

Different types of seaweed are commonly used in Korean cooking. Korean supermarkets sell bags of fresh, green seaweed and dried seaweed, too.

Seaweed is very nutritious. It contains lots of vitamins and minerals, which is why seaweed soup is fed to pregnant

Muyokguk, or seaweed soup, is always present at birthday celebrations. It tastes sweet, salty, bitter, and spicy.

First Birthday Celebrations

A child's first birthday is an important event in Korea. Parents throw big parties in which twelve different varieties of rice cakes are served.

Along with the rice cakes, a book, money, dried fruit, a knife, a bow and arrow, and a needle and thread are placed in front of the birthday child. Then everyone watches to see what item the child will pick up first. According to tradition, the child's selection predicts his or her future. If the child picks up the book the child is destined to be a scholar. The money means the child will be wealthy. The knife means the child is destined to be a good cook, while the fruit means the child will have many children. The needle and thread stands for long life. The bow and arrow means the child will be a warrior.

women in Korea. New mothers eat seaweed soup and no other soup for three weeks after giving birth in an effort to fortify their breast milk. So, indirectly, the soup is the first soup Korean babies eat. Eating it on birthdays reminds Koreans of their mothers and the love and caring they gave them. "No birthday," Lee insists, "could go by without the soothing liquid of seaweed soup."[21]

Besides seaweed, the soup contains chicken, garlic, green onions, soy sauce, sesame oil, sesame seeds, and tofu or soybean curd. Sometimes sweet and sticky rice balls are added. The soup smells faintly of the ocean, and tastes spicy, salty, sweet, and slightly bitter.

Seaweed Soup

Seaweed or kelp is available at some supermarkets and in most Asian grocery stores. It is usually sold in dried form. You can add shredded cooked chicken or beef to the soup.

Ingredients
1 ounce dried kelp
4 cups chicken, beef, or vegetable broth
1 teaspoon minced garlic
1 tablespoon sesame oil
1 tablespoon soy sauce

Directions
1. Soak the seaweed in water until it becomes soft. Drain the seaweed and rinse it to remove any sand. Squeeze out excess liquid.
2. Put the seaweed in a pot with all the other ingredients. Cook the soup over medium heat until it boils. Lower the heat and simmer for about 10 minutes.
Serves 4-6.

The Noodle Banquet

Soup is also an important part of wedding dinners, as are chestnuts and dried fruit. Traditionally, the last two are thrown at the bride by her mother-in-law. The bride catches as many nuts and fruits as she can in her skirt. The number she catches symbolizes the number of children she will have.

The soup served at Korean weddings also has special meaning. Korean weddings are usually huge feasts

Guksu, noodle soup, has a special meaning at Korean weddings and is always included. Eating the soup is a way to wish the bride and groom a happy life.

in which dozens of dishes are served. The menu varies, but guksu (KOOK-soo), or noodle soup, is always part of the celebration. In fact, Korean wedding dinners are called guksu sang (KOOK-soo-sang) or noodle banquets. And, it is common for older Koreans to greet unmarried family members by asking when they will be invited to a noodle banquet.

Chinese merchants brought noodles to Korea around A.D. 100. They also brought the Chinese belief that long noodles symbolize long life, which Koreans adopted.

Korean wedding soup contains soft, chewy wheat

Special Teas

Koreans say that tea strengthens their bodies and clears their minds. Barley tea, which is made with barley and hot water, is probably the most popular tea in Korea. It is served in Korean restaurants in much the same way that water is served in the United States. Koreans believe barley tea stimulates the appetite and reduces fatigue.

Rice tea, which is also very popular, is believed to promote good digestion. It is often drunk after a meal. Rice tea is made by pouring boiling water onto the rice that sticks to the bottom of a pot.

Sesame tea, made by pouring boiling water over powder made of ground sesame seeds, is also believed to improve health. Brides often drink it before their wedding. It is believed to have a calming effect on the body as well as promoting healthy skin and hair.

noodles, cut extra long to represent longevity. They are boiled in beef broth with vegetables, chili powder, eggs, garlic, and soy sauce, and topped with dried seaweed. Eating the soup is a symbolic way for guests to wish the newly married couple a long and happy life together.

Whether its guksu for weddings, muyokguk for birthday parties, ttokguk for Lunar New Year's, or songpyeon for Korean Thanksgiving, food plays an important part in Korean life. Special food with special meanings make Korean celebrations memorable. Without them, Korean holidays and special events would not be as interesting or unique.

Mass (weight)

1 ounce (oz.)	= 28.0 grams (g)
8 ounces	= 227.0 grams
1 pound (lb.) or 16 ounces	= 0.45 kilograms (kg)
2.2 pounds	= 1.0 kilogram

Liquid Volume

1 teaspoon (tsp.)	= 5.0 milliliters (ml)
1 tablespoon (tbsp.)	= 15.0 milliliters
1 fluid ounce (oz.)	= 30.0 milliliters
1 cup (c.)	= 240 milliliters
1 pint (pt.)	= 480 milliliters
1 quart (qt.)	= 0.96 liters (l)
1 gallon (gal.)	= 3.84 liters

Pan Sizes

8- inch cake pan	= 20 x 4-centimeter cake pan
9-inch cake pan	= 23 x 3.5-centimeter cake pan
11 x 7-inch baking pan	= 28 x 18-centimeter baking pan
13 x 9-inch baking pan	= 32.5 x 23-centimeter baking pan
9 x 5-inch loaf pan	= 23 x 13-centimeter loaf pan
2-quart casserole	= 2-liter casserole

Temperature

212° F	= 100° C (boiling point of water)
225° F	= 110° C
250° F	= 120° C
275° F	= 135° C
300° F	= 150° C
325° F	= 160° C
350° F	= 180° C
375° F	= 190° C
400° F	= 200° C

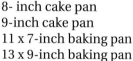

Length

1/4 inch (in.)	= 0.6 centimeters (cm)
1/2 inch	= 1.25 centimeters
1 inch	= 2.5 centimeters

Notes

Chapter 1: The Heart of Korean Cooking

1. Cecila Hae-Jin Lee, *Eating Korean*. Hoboken, NJ: John Wiley & Sons, 2005, p. 12.

2. Chang Sun-Young, *A Korean Mother's Cooking Notes*. Seoul, South Korea: Ewha Woman's University Press, 1997, p. 21.

3. Hi Soo Shin Hepinstall, *Growing Up in a Korean Kitchen*. Berkeley, CA: Ten Speed Press, 2001, p. 110.

4. Jane Daniels Lear, "A Taste of Korea," *Gourmet*, March 2009, p. 101.

5. Hepinstall, *Growing Up in a Korean Kitchen*, p. 94.

6. Hepinstall, *Growing Up in a Korean Kitchen*, p. 24.

Chapter 2: A Delicious Balance

7. Quoted in Jamie Purviance, "Seoul Food," *Bon Appetit*, July 2009, p. 94.

8. Sun-Young, *A Korean Mother's Cooking Notes*, p.41.

9. Quoted in Lauren Bianchi, "Korean Cuisine, Culture Becomes an Acquired Taste," *Daily Herald* (Arlington, Illinois), May 23, 2001, p. 3.

10. Jonathan Frye, "Banchan," *Saveur*, January/February 2010, p. 45.

11. Kristin Johannsen, "Across Korea with Chopsticks," *World and I*, January 2004, p. 124.

12. Purviance, "Seoul Food," p. 94.

Chapter 3: A Snacker's Paradise

13. Cathy Rose A. Garcia, "Seoul Food Trips," People Recruit People. www.peoplerecruit.com/e_page/index.php?move_dir=board&sub_page=view&board_no=265.

14. Matthew Bell, "Korean Cuisine," PRI's The World. www.pri.org/ theworld/?q=node/14804.

15. Robyn Lee, "Snapshots from South Korea: Hotteok Two Ways," May 31, 2009. Serious Eats. www.seriouseats.com/2009/05/ snapshots_from_south_korea_hotteok_two_ways_insadong_ seoul.html.

16. Quoted in Julia Moskin, "South Korea Campaigns to Spice up the World with Kimchi," September 24, 2009, National Restaurant News. www.nrn.com/offthewire.aspx?menu_id=1370&id =373334.

17. "Fish Noodles on a Stick," March 2, 2009, ZenKimchi Korean Food Journal. www.zenkimchi.com/FoodJournal/archives/category/ street-food.

Chapter 4: Meaningful Foods

18. Lee, *Eating Korean*, p. 202.

19. Lee, *Eating Korean*, p. 201.

20. Hepinstall, *Growing Up in a Korean Kitchen.* p. 231.

21. Lee, *Eating Korean*, p. 207.

Glossary

Allies: The name given to the group of nations that fought against Germany, Italy, and Japan in World War II.

banchan: Side dishes of vegetables, kimchi, and other foods that are served at every meal.

bap: The Korean word for rice.

bibimbap: A rice, vegetable, and meat dish.

brine: A saltwater solution in which food may be preserved.

broth: The liquid in which bones, meat, fish, or vegetables have been boiled.

bulgogi: Thin strips of barbecued beef.

Chuseok: A three-day harvest moon festival similar to Thanksgiving.

fermented: Having gone through a chemical process in which bacteria breaks down sugars to produce acids or alcohols that make food taste sour.

herbalists: People who study herbs and their medicinal properties.

kalbi: Barbecued beef ribs.

kelp: A type of seaweed.

kimchi: A spicy fermented vegetable dish.

merchants: Traders or salespeople.

pajeon: A popular pancake made with green onions.

peninsula: Land that is surrounded by water on three sides.

pojangmachas: Food carts or stalls that sell snacks.

probiotics: Bacteria that help the body by taking up space that would otherwise house disease-causing bacteria.

Sol-nal: The Lunar New Year.

songpyeon: Half-moon-shaped rice cakes eaten on Chuseok.

For Further Exploration

Books

Okwha Chung and Judy Monroe, *Cooking the Korean Way*. Minneapolis: Lerner, 2003. A simple Korean cookbook for kids.

Devagi Sanmugam and Marijke Den Ouden, *Fun with Asian Food: A Kid's Cookbook*. Singapore: Periplus Editions, 2005. This cookbook offers simple recipes from many Asian nations, including Korea.

Tara Walters, *North Korea*. New York: Children's Press, 2008. Discusses why North Korea is a closed society and what life is like there.

Walters, *South Korea*. New York: Children's Press, 2008. Looks at South Korea's history, traditions, and popular culture.

Web Sites

K Bears "South Korea" (www.kbears.com/skorea/information.html). This Web site for kids gives statistics about South Korea, information about its history, photos, a map, the national anthem, and great links.

Kids-Online "South Korea" (www.kids-online.net/world/skorea.html). Two Korean children tell about their country. One gives his e-mail address. There is also a picture of the Korean flag and a recording of the national anthem.

National Geographic Kids "South Korea" (http://kids.nationalgeographic.com/Places/Find/South-korea). This Web site provides lots of information about South Korea's history, geography, wildlife, culture, government, and economics. It has a map, pictures, a video, and an e-card.

PBS.org "Hidden Korea" (http://www.pbs.org/hiddenkorea/index.htm). This Web site gives information about South Korea's history, culture, and religion. There is a section on Chuseok, and lots of information about Korean food. It has beautiful photos.

Yahoo Kids "World Factbook North Korea" (http://kids.yahoo.com/reference/world-factbook/country/kn—Korea%2C+North#main). Information on North Korea, including facts about its history, government, economy, military, and a picture of the flag.

Index

Picture credits

About the Author

Barbara Sheen is the author of more than 50 books for young people. She lives in New Mexico with her family. In her spare time, she likes to swim, garden, walk, and read. Of course, she loves to cook!